The Depression Code

How to Get Over Depression and Anxiety

Jack Wilson

Copyright © 2019 Jack Wilson

All rights reserved.

ISBN-13: 978-1-0707-3650-1

© COPYRIGHT 2019 BY **JACK WILSON** - ALL RIGHTS RESERVED.

The content contained within this book may not be reproduced, duplicated or transmitted without direct written permission from the author or the publisher.

Under no circumstances will any blame or legal responsibility be held against the publisher, or author, for any damages, reparation, or monetary loss due to the information contained within this book. Either directly or indirectly.

Legal Notice:
This book is copyright protected. This book is only for personal use. You cannot amend, distribute, sell, use, quote or paraphrase any part, or the content within this book, without the consent of the author or publisher.

Disclaimer Notice:
Please note the information contained within this document is for educational and entertainment purposes only. All effort has been executed to present accurate, up to date, and reliable, complete information. No warranties of any kind are declared or implied. Readers acknowledge that the author is not engaging in the rendering of legal, financial, medical or professional advice. The content within this book has been derived from various sources. Please consult a licensed professional before attempting any techniques outlined in this book.

By reading this book, the reader agrees that under no circumstances is the author responsible for any losses, direct or indirect, which are incurred as a result of the use of information contained within this document, including, but not limited to, — errors, omissions, or inaccuracies..

CONTENTS

	Introduction	1
1	What is Depression?	3
2	Recognizing the Symptoms	7
3	Seeking Professional Help	10
4	Cognitive Behavioral Therapy (CBT)	14
5	Day to Day Living: The Recovery Period	17
6	Dealing with the Stigma of Mental Illness	22
7	Wellness tips	27
	Conclusion	33

INTRODUCTION

Depression is a condition that is an all-encompassing illness. It wreaks havoc on our bodies, minds, and souls. Depression is something that we may struggle with for a while and then decide to give in to despair. Having a depressive episode is one of the most difficult things I have struggled with through the years. But through it all, I have recovered from a difficult journey with depression that has followed me all my life. Through my experience, I want to share how a person can endure the hardships of depression and come out victorious on the other side.

This book is entitled Depression Code, and it is just that: it is a code that enables you to figure out and understand what depression is, the symptoms, and how to cope with the illness. We will also explore how you can live a healthy and normal life while dealing with depression.

While you might think that it is impossible to keep going with this condition, I urge you to consider how you can make a life that is full of joy, even in the midst of sadness. Think about how you can use positive energy to lighten your day and become a happier person. Don't allow the shadows to overtake you, and don't think that you have to stay there. Instead, find ways to cope and live in wellness. That is what this book is for. I want to present an account of depression in the life of an ordinary individual and prescribe advice that will enable you to live meaningfully in the midst of a difficult time.

There are seven chapters in this book. First, I explain what depression is and give you information about it that includes symptoms. Then, I'll talk about ways to seek professional assistance from a medical doctor or psychiatrist. Next, cognitive behavioral therapy (CBT) and creating a wellness plan for your life are discussed. Following this chapter, I will deal with the recovery stage of handling mental illness, as well as the stigma that is attached to it. Finally, there are some final wellness tips to help you on the road to recovery.

Let us now crack the Depression Code and find ways of living and thriving with mental health wellness.

1 WHAT IS DEPRESSION?

In this chapter, the symptoms of the illness and how it is manifested are outlined. I will talk about how depression has affected my life and how the depression diagnosis came about for me. I want to tell my story of depression and how I was able to overcome and live with it.

What is Depression?

Depression affects millions of Americans every year. It is one of the most common forms of mental illness. Many people die each day because they do not receive the proper mental healthcare. These individuals require medical attention to surmount the challenges in their lives because this disease is killing them. More people are feeling hopeless and unable to find help, so they commit suicide. Suicides have increased by 30% since 1996, according to a study from the Center for Disease Control (CDC) in the United States.

Depressive disorders touch the lives of everyone involved. It is a pervasive illness that affects a person's ability not only to think and reason but also to function. It is an all-encompassing disorder that has impacted Americans due to financial difficulties and relationship woes, among other reasons. And, as more individuals are getting treatment for mental illness, there is hope that people can receive help and healing.

Depression ranges from feeling low and gloomy to not being

able to get out of bed in the morning. When a person experiences depression, their body seemingly slows down and leads to mind fog. Because the condition impacts the brain, they are not able to cognitively function well. They can barely walk or move around because their whole body is affected. When a person is depressed, they cannot motivate themselves to get out of difficult places. They feel stuck where they are and unable to get out of the hell that is being depressed. It is a deep trough that sucks all the energy out of life, where you are unable to see the light of day because your soul is downcast, and you cannot experience joy or peace. Every part of you is stuck deep in a purgatory of emotion an distress. These feelings can last from a few hours to a couple days to weeks or even months. It depends on what day it is and depending on how you deal with it, you may stay in that dark place for a while.

I would like to tell my story as a survivor of mental illness. I have had depression my whole life, and it has caused me to see the light and experience the serenity of knowing that I am loved and that I have never walked alone with this illness. Guided by faith in God, I believe that every step has been directed toward a greater happiness that I never thought I could have before. I want to begin my journey with my childhood because that's where my depression began.

Religious Family: Pressure and Anxiety

I grew up as a son of religious parents and I was taught from an early age that God sees everything we do and hears everything we say. I was convinced since I was a child that one day we will return to God for judgement, and that we should always ask him for guidance and seek his forgiveness for our sins.

Growing up in a religious family, I felt intense pressure to perform, to be a "good boy," and to behave as if I were the best child. Additionally, I was the first son in my family, which made it even more difficult, because I knew that I had to be good. I constantly thought that I had to perform for everyone. That made me into a perfectionist. Often, I would criticize myself and suffer intense stress because I thought that I had to do everything perfectly.

In school, I pressured myself even more. I cried every time I got a "B" on an assignment. I always had to get straight A's. I idolized the "A" because I thought that I always needed to get an "A" on every assignment, regardless of what it was. I poured myself into my studies because that is where I could develop an identity for myself. It was only through that experience that I was able to feel as if I was accepted and validated. If I got an "A," I would feel as though I had attained success and that I was doing well.

What I didn't realize was how much this made me miserable. I felt so empty most days. My energy level was low all the time. I hardly got any exercise, and I was always falling asleep as soon as I got home. I did my homework and completed my duties faithfully. I stayed up late to study and felt that this was the only way I could find happiness.

Most days, I remained by myself. I wouldn't talk to anyone at school. I had no friends, and I was completely antisocial. My introversion caused me to look deeper within myself to find meaning and purpose in my life, because I was unable to find it in other things.

I was exhausted every day, and I felt oppressed by the negative energy that seemed to consume me. I was unhappy, I was suffering from chronic depression, and it was difficult to understand what was happening to me. I didn't realize how much it was taking over my life. It caused me the greatest amount of challenge and anxiety, so I constantly suffered from pain that inflicted harm upon my soul. Darkness and turmoil constantly surrounded me.

Then one day, it took over me. I was overcome by the inner demons that spoke to me. I stayed up one night until nearly three in the morning. I was desperate to escape from my situation. I wanted to get out as fast as I could. I wanted to get out of the shadows of my mind, the chasm of darkness that infected my whole being. I wanted to fly away to New Zealand, so I imagined myself flying away to New Zealand and discovering the land where the Lord of the Rings was filmed. The next day, I drove to school with my brother. I was overtaken by emotion and felt extremely out of it. I was drunk with the desire to fly away to New Zealand. It was welling up inside of me. Manically, I spoke to people and bragged about how I was going to fly in a helicopter and go to New Zealand. People knew there was some kind of problem and that I was hallucinating.

That whole day seemed like a vague blur. I was deep in the chasm of my mind but externalizing an inner reality that was haunted by demons. It was an incredible place to be. My dad took me home that day. I vomited so much. I was sick. I needed to get help. My parents were there to love and support me. I can never forget how much they cared for me, how they walked me through that time, how they cried with me and calmed me through the dark pain that was depression.

Soon after, I was checked into a psychiatric ward of a nearby hospital and stayed one week. It was there that I learned what I was dealing with, the disorder that I had: manic depression, which was a form of depression that affected the emotions. During that phase I realized what I was dealing with in the manic depression diagnosis. I learned about how to deal with depression and what I could do to get out of the deep holes in my mind. I could identify the early warning signs, when I was about to go off the deep end, and how to direct my thoughts in a positive direction so that I could deal with the challenging emotions that could have taken over my life.

The diagnosis was the beginning of the journey of treatment, healing, and recovery. It was one part of the adventure that I will never forget, but it was necessary so that I could be the man I am today, living with the shadows of mental illness behind me. It changed and transformed my life. I am no longer the same person because I was able to survive one of the darkest moments of my life, in the depths of my depression. But by the grace of God, I was able to exit and come out of that trough stronger and more capable than ever.

2 RECOGNIZING THE SYMPTOMS

In this chapter, I will discuss how to recognize the symptoms of depression by using my personal anecdote.

When I went to the hospital, I found out how to detect the symptoms of depression in myself, which enabled me to offer some prescriptive advice for recognizing if a person is in a depressed state. The information I acquired from the therapists and psychiatrists at the hospital allowed me to come up with ways of coping with the symptoms of depression that I still use today.

Symptoms of Depression

Often, we don't realize that we are drifting into a depressive state until it is too late and then we are deep in it. Before I became educated in mental health through the various experiences I had, I tended to fall into depression and stay there without realizing that I had gotten there in the first place. I didn't know how to recognize the early warning signs of depression and whether I was drifting into the danger zone.

Early Warning Signs

Becoming depressed is a process and it usually starts with changes in a person's routine. If things get too out of balance in a person's daily life, things start to tip over and depression can easily get in the way. One of the most important things that can change is sleep. When a person is sleeping too much or too little, things start to get strange. You start feeling too tired to do things. Your energy level tanks and then you recognize that you are starting to lose it. Sleep is one of the most important aspects of our lives, because our body and mind need to restore themselves following a long day. When the body does not get rest, it can easily shift into a dangerous area, where there is no energy and that can cause us to become depressed. This was one way I recognized that my depression was beginning. When my sleep cycle started getting off, my tendency to get depressed greatly increased.

Second, when you start decreasing your time spent with people, you are starting to slip into depression. People who suffer from depression often do so in isolation and silence. They don't want others to know they are feeling depressed, so they ghost and get out of others' lives. This causes them to feel empty inside. But social isolation only exacerbates the problem, because the more time you spend alone, the lonelier and more depressed you feel. Moreover, this can cause a person to go off the edge and end up depressed.

Third, when a person's appetite shifts and they no longer eat well or eat too much, things also start to go awry with mood and emotions. Because our body is either taking in too many nutrients or not enough, energy levels start to tank and cause us to feel immensely tired and unable to tackle everyday situations. This leads to a depressed mindset that is sluggish and unable to concentrate or get things done normally.

Fourthly, whenever we start to feel immensely tired or burned out, the body starts to break down. Physically, we are exhausted from everything and cannot function as well as we could before, so we start to lose more energy. When this happens, we can easily enter into a phase of depression where we are no longer able to move our bodies. We feel stuck and slowed down by the things that have caused us to feel this way. Consequently, we feel sad and down because we are not able to do the things we were able to do before.

The Feelings of Depression

These early warning signs lead us to enter depression where we feel enclosed by its dark walls. These feelings shut us out of others' lives and cause us to be down on ourselves. We feel the sting of perfectionism as it pierces our sides and leads us into deeper depression. The waves of negativity infect our thinking in ways that were previously unknown. Then, we are unable to see past the negativity. Our minds are clouded with it so that we are unable to cope. It is as if we have been shut out of the light forever. Those moments of depression are difficult, because they are life-sucking, literally taking our breath away. We can no longer function, so we stay at home. We take off work, because we don't want to go out. We don't want others to experience our depression. Instead, we would prefer to suffer in silence and isolation, deep within ourselves, because we have pride that we can overcome it alone only by entering a profound introspection of ourselves.

My Experience of Depression

In the deep introspection of my life, I have experienced the deep chasm of depression. It is life-altering. When you are depressed, you can feel it taking every ounce of energy from you and you don't want to go anywhere but remain in the darkness. But then, you also want to fight for your life to get out. Deep within that self-analysis is an evil spirit that wants you to stay there, that wants you to die and suffer forever. It is a type of hell that people who are depressed experience. They listen to the lies of this evil spirit, thinking that they will not be able to get out of it; that there is no way out. Whenever I felt depressed, I had to get out of the mindset that the depression is going to take over my life. In the moments I feel depressed, I remind myself, "You have overcome so much. Before this, you were able to conquer the depression. Don't think that this moment is any different. Keep fighting. You have to go on. Although you feel that this moment is a time of mourning, tomorrow you will be thriving and dancing!"

The way to deal with depression is to fight. Fight, I tell you, fight! You cannot passively expect to get out of depression. Don't allow the lies of the evil spirits and demons within it to take over your life. There is nothing worse than allowing those things to cause you anxiety and pain deeper than the depression itself. Depression is an illness that can only be fought. When you experience it, you have to fight for your life, because truly, at times, it can seem like a matter of life or death. Depression is a dangerous place to be, but only when you can move beyond the hopeless feelings and low energy can you overcome that place that grieves your spirit.

My journey of fighting through depression started with my diagnosis. Progressively over time, I was able to discover what I needed to do to get better. Over the course of about ten years, I journeyed through to get to a better place of healing and restoration. I would fell and got back up again many times. Occasionally, I would be depressed and feel down and want to stay home all the time. I would feel a great weight of pressure that was crushing me. It was suffocating me so that it was so hard to breathe. The strains of depression can make a person go into a deep chasm within themselves. With God's grace, I have never entered into the chamber of suicidal thoughts that could destroy me forever. Instead, I have been spared much of the inner demons that can cause a person to fly off the handle, because the hopeless feelings of it can overpower and conquer. My life has been a testament of healing and recovery that has allowed me to come out triumphant over the inner turmoil caused by depression.

3 SEEKING PROFESSIONAL HELP

In this chapter, I will talk about how I sought help from a psychiatrist and counselor and was able to get professional assistance for my mental illness.

One of the biggest lies people believe when they have a mental illness is that they have to have it all together. They think they can get assistance without going to a doctor or psychiatrist. These individuals have a great deal of self-reliance and feel they must face the elements all by themselves. They never bother going to see a doctor to get medicine for whatever ailment is bothering them. Men are more likely to be this way and are less likely to seek mental health help when they need it most. The rise of male suicides far exceeds that of women in the United States today. No wonder so many people are not getting the help they need! They aren't looking for it. Instead, they pursue their own path without regard to what they really need: someone who can listen to and help them.

When I was first diagnosed with depression, I believed I needed someone to help me. I was compliant with my parents and doctors and didn't want to question it. I knew that doctors and psychiatrists were helpful people and that they were the ones who were going to get me where I needed to be. I trusted them and believed that modern medicine could get me the guidance I required.

Week after week, I went to see the psychiatrist to help me with my illness. I had to try different doctors to get it right. There were a couple of terrible doctors who did not help me at all. One of the doctors saw me in the hospital. What was his solution to my problem? Drugs. He gave me so many drugs that I could hardly function, let alone get up out of bed every day. He was not helpful. One our family friends said, "Get away from that doctor. He won't help you at all." So, my parents stopped my appointments. It made a huge difference. Soon, we were able to find a medical professional who made the biggest impact on my life in healing from the disorder. He was a bit older than others, nearing retirement. But it was amazing to see how this doctor interacted with me.

He was special. You don't normally find this kind of caring, gentle, nurturing, and sensitive demeanor from most physicians, but that's the way he was. He always smiled at me when I walked into the office and was always willing to listen to me, even when I felt I was going through a difficult time. Dr. S. knew I had high goals for my life. He knew that I wanted to get into higher education and get a terminal degree in an advanced subject. I told him that I wanted to become a doctor one day and go to a prestigious school. I didn't want to back down on that goal, although I had a mental illness. I also didn't want to allow my illness to impact my life, because I could not just give up. It was not in my blood. My family never gave up, so I wouldn't allow a difficult circumstance to deter me. Dr. S. saw how much I was persevering through my last year of high school and he stated that he was proud of me. He always encouraged me and let me know that I would be able to live a normal life. Dr S. saw the progress I made, and he knew that I get better within a year or two, and it was amazing how he got me there.

How did I start recovering? Healing began with medical consultations with my psychiatrist, Dr. S. The doctor tried numerous formulas for medication.

Disclaimer: There is no magical formula for medicine. Everyone has different body chemistry. Each person's body reacts differently to different medicines, and no two persons will be in the same. I cannot prescribe a medication to suit your situation. You must consult a psychiatrist to help you. Dr. S. tried different medications with me. These medicines had various side effects. Some of the medicines, especially the antidepressants and antiseizure medications, caused me to feel manic and relapse into symptoms that I had before, so we discarded those. It took over a year to get where I needed to be. I continued to consult with my doctor when I was in college. During that time that I was able to develop a wellness plan. My doctor guided me, not just in prescribing medicine, but also in getting me to feel well and do things that encouraged a healthy lifestyle. He always told me to eat a good diet and to exercise, so I did. Dr. S. helped me manage my stress so that I could do all the things I needed to succeed academically.

Seeing my doctor every week was crucial in getting me where I wanted to be. I was not ashamed. I allowed myself to submit to the authority of medical professionals who had much greater knowledge about mental health. It made a difference. I think a lot of people don't seek medical attention because they are too proud. They think that they can do it alone by reading a self-help book or using another resource. Professional help is actually a necessity in many situations. Stop trying to be strong. Seek medical guidance from someone who understands your condition better than you do. Allow them to help you achieve your dreams. It will be one of the best decisions you'll ever make.

Choosing the Right Doctor

Choose a medical professional who will listen to you. Find someone who will hear you out on all the issues you face. Going to a doctor who only offers advice without listening to you is counterproductive and will not help you. Find a doctor who will listen to what you have to say, because your experience of the illness is an important part of your treatment plan. A doctor should not drug you to the max. There are plenty of physicians who put their patients on as many prescriptions as possible. Avoid them. Realize that you cannot yield to the authority of someone who will to cause you cognitive impairment and irreversible memory damage. Locate a doctor who will be on-call in case there is an emergency and who will be available when you need them, because that will help you endure whatever crisis may arise. One last bit of advice, stick with the doctor that meets your needs and comes up with a treatment plan that will help you.

Try Talk Therapy

In addition to your psychiatrist, the choice of a therapist is important. In many cases, I would say this is an equally essential consideration. Often, it is helpful to see a therapist who is of the same gender because that can help ease any communication burdens that may cross those lines.

Talk therapy is a proven method to help with depression and anxiety disorders. When I was dealing with my depression and anxiety, I went to see a therapist who was also able to help me through those periods and develop positive thinking techniques that helped me out of the difficult thinking I had as a result of depression. I would say, however, that talk therapy is not an absolute necessity for treatment for depression. Seeing a therapist is something that you can do whenever you feel like it and perhaps only at times of deep depression.

It is not mandatory to see a therapist. There are other ways to get help, including social therapy. When a person spends time with their friends, they can experience happiness and comfort because they feel that they are with people that understand and love them. That is important in this world. Having friends makes a difference in how we live. People with depressive illnesses can benefit from having a few close friendships, which can be life-giving and life-changing in the midst of hard times. They can be a vital source of energy in the middle of depression, which is a time in which many people choose to close themselves inward.

Conclusion

At the end of the day, what is crucial is your wellness. Maybe you are enduring a depressive episode now and need help. Go and seek the help you need. Don't procrastinate any longer. Find a doctor who can give you the medical advice necessary to manage your symptoms. Sometimes we may need medication to help our bodies get back on the right track. In many cases, we may have to go on medication for the long-term. That does not make us weak or unable to handle things. Instead, it demonstrates maturity and proactivity, which are necessary to live a successful life.

Find someone you can talk to about your depression. That may be a counselor or therapist or a trusted friend that you can talk to about any matter. In any case, it is vital that you find someone who can listen to you and your concerns. Don't try to do it yourself any longer. Receive the assistance that could save your life. It is the most important thing you can do for yourself today.

4 COGNITIVE BEHAVIORAL THERAPY (CBT)

In this chapter, I will explain about how I was able to seek CBT from my therapist and how that process led to my healing and recovery.

My doctor mentioned Cognitive Behavioral Therapy (CBT) as a possible route for my condition, which is a method that can help you with your thinking. I went through a few sessions with my doctor, which helped me later. Different things stood out to me, which made me value the time that I spent with him.

CBT is a Way to Reprogram Our Minds

The first thing that I realized about CBT was that it was a way that I could reprogram my mind to think in a different way. Before this, I was intensely negative toward myself and I always had streams of negative thoughts that became so uncontrollable that they had a "snowball effect" and kept rolling and rolling. My thoughts were a mess and in a jumble, so that I could no longer think clearly but also I was in a web of anxiety and nervousness. I was a wreck. Through studying CBT with my doctor, I realized that what had to change in my life was my way of thinking.

CBT changes your mindset because you focus on the here and now. You stop and hold the thought that is precipitating into a mess of jumbled sentences in your mind. When you use CBT, you can stop yourself from flying off the handle, because you understand what you need to do to get out of despair. You also proactively steer clear of those dangerous thoughts. I recall one algebra teacher, who used to tell us "Danger! Danger!" to help us watch for making careless calculation mistakes. When you use CBT, you can stop whenever danger is close and get out of harm's way, because you know how to do it. Everything starts with a change of mindset.

CBT Enables You to Relax

The second thing I learned about CBT was that it was a way to relax. It's like meditating. When you use CBT, you calm yourself and "feel" your thoughts. It also helps you when you feel anxious or depressed. I noticed this when I sat in a chair and was using CBT. It was an effective experience, because it helped me to reframe my mind so that I could relax. I didn't think about the cares and worries of my life. I simply released those thoughts that were keeping me captive and let myself go. It helped me surrender my thoughts and release the strains that were causing my pain and anxiety. It did wonders for my mental health.

CBT is Temporary but Leads to Long-term Benefits

Most CBT is temporary and only lasts a short while, from a few weeks to a few months. It is an intensive time for the patient, as they are reprogramming their thought patterns, but as they go through it, they can enjoy the aftereffects. While talking to the therapist, they can train their minds to think a certain way all the time. Once they have mastered this technique, then they are free to do what they want, and they don't need the support of the therapist any longer.

How does it work? CBT becomes ingrained in the mind and gives the person habits that stick for life. When you train your mind to live in the present moment, turn away from negative thought patterns, and free yourself of the anxiety within, it helps you a lot in life. You feel free of the bondage of despair that exists within depression and anxiety. One of the greatest aspects of CBT is once you have mastered the basics is that they never leave you. The habits and thoughts cultivated in the recovery stage will follow you and enable you to permanently heal from the negative thought patterns that had a stronghold over your life.

When to Recommend CBT for Your Treatment Plan

Your doctor may recommend CBT to your therapist. Short intensive sessions for a few weeks may be required. You will likely have to see your therapist a few times a week for several weeks. CBT does require some time and expense to the patient, but it is well worth the effort and money to get you back on the right track. CBT helps you cope with the symptoms of depression when you are in the thick of it, as well as when you're feeling well and have no problems.

Primarily, CBT will be used as a means to treat the depression or anxiety you may be experiencing at a given time. CBT is a great short-term treatment plan for your disorder that may produce long-term results. In some cases, it has enabled people to go off medicine for a period. However, it is not guaranteed to provide you with complete restoration; it is only one step to recovering fully from the illness that will lead to long-term wellness.

Conclusion

You may think CBT is an appropriate solution for your depression. CBT is going to dramatically improve your confidence in yourself in a positive way. Positive thinking will impact how you relate to others and will enable you to live a life full of productivity and joy. You will be happy to see how you can recover from the blues. It will become a new way of thinking that you hadn't tried before. But once you have tried it, you won't go back. It's like the Point of No Return. You will experience freedom and peace which will last for the rest of your life. Coping with depression will become thriving. Then, you will know what it really means to finally be free. It will be at that point that you will have found meaning and significance again in your life. You will able to discover what it means to live again. Again, seek the help you need, where you need it. Don't underestimate it. Your life depends on receiving help from others and it can prolong your life.

5 DAY TO DAY LIVING: THE RECOVERY PERIOD

Day to day, living with mental illness is a very hard thing. It is not easy to find ways to deal with the illness, especially when you are in the heat of it. When you experience depression or an anxiety attack, your whole world can seem as if it is turned upside down. Nothing seems to be falling into place. You feel unbalanced and off-kilter and everything around you causes you to feel down. When you're in that place, you feel trapped, almost as if you cannot get out. I've been there; it was one of the most difficult moments of my life. Perhaps you also have been depressed for a while and are unsure how to get out of your situation. The struggle may be as simple or as hard as getting out of bed every day. This chapter is about my road to recovery and how a person can recover from depressive episodes.

Recovery Phase: Out of the Hospital

As I mentioned previously, I had to go to the hospital when I was 17 years old. The period following my hospitalization was filled with ups and downs. Sometimes, I felt joyful, and other times, I felt very sad. During that time, I was sluggish and felt down a lot. It was hard to function for the rest of my senior year. Because I was on so much medication, I had no idea how I could get out of it. I didn't feel like myself. In fact, I felt like I was constantly in a trance-like state. I had to recover a lot of things in my life during that time - how to function in school and how to get along with my peers, among other things. It took an entire year to get back to where I wanted to be. But in the end, I graduated and had a 3.98 GPA. I only got one "B" in a class. I achieved my goal to be admitted to a prestigious school, Emory University, although I went to another lesser-known undergraduate college in Georgia instead.

Phase 2: University (1-4 years later)

After I graduated from high school, I went to college close to my house, where my family lived. It was helpful because I could go home on the weekend if necessary. I went home frequently and spent more time with my family. I went to a religious institution. It was there that I was able to find faith in God more clearly than before, but I still struggled with my self-concept and esteem. I still got sick before tests and got incredibly nervous and anxious before exams. I studied so hard in college and was still not able to get all A's. In the end, my GPA was an A- with a 3.70 GPA, but I was satisfied because I graduated with honors.

During my time at university, I had some hard experiences, as well. There were phases where I was concerned about my faith and my grades and all those things. I also saw a therapist at the college who helped me through different difficulties. In addition, I continued to go with my parents to see my psychiatrist, who gave me months of prescriptions, because I was doing much better. I gained some stability in my moods and felt better overall, although I still felt depressed and anxious occasionally. Sometimes, it was excruciatingly difficult. My sleeping was off frequently. The stresses of university life created a lot of hardship for me as a person who was dealing with mental illness. With the free time that I had, I wanted to spend it sleeping or studying. Actually, I didn't think I had a healthy lifestyle while in college. It was a typical student way of living, although I didn't drink or smoke because those things were not allowed on campus.

In the end, however, I succeeded. I never gave up. My doctor helped me through it. He assisted me with coping strategies to deal with the various stressors of college life. Dr. S. realized l that I wanted to do some amazing things. He knew that I could do whatever I set my mind to, because I was guided by my faith and that this would enable me to do everything. Although Dr. S. did not guide me by his faith, he gave me some important steps to leading a healthy and happy life. I will never forget how he reassured me, "You can live a normal and healthy life." It made a big difference, as I saw that indeed I could surpass all the expectations I had of myself.

In 2010, I graduated from college. I knew that I could accomplish my dreams and that from that point onward, I would be able to do anything because I was guided by my faith and confidence that anything is possible.

Phase 3: The Past Decade (2010-2019): Healing

The past decade has been filled with ups and downs, but it has been a time full of healing that I cannot fully explain. I was able to fully recover from the effects of depression. I will briefly summarize how that all came about.

After I graduated from college, I moved to France and worked as an assistant English teacher. Then, I wanted to get a Ph.D. in French from a prominent university in the U.S. I was accepted to a Ph.D. program at an Ivy League university. I went there and had a difficult time. I struggled with depression and anxiety. It was one of the hardest moments of my life, as well. I sought treatment from a psychiatrist who gave me antidepressants and an anti-anxiety medication. I left the Ph.D. program after one year and moved to Boston, where I worked as an ESL teacher. That was another time of healing. I experienced so many amazing moments after that, along with a community of friends that gave me a place where I could live and thrive.

After that, I moved back to France to work in a university as an English teacher. I wanted to get into education as a professor. That was my goal: to pursue a life in education as a researcher and teacher, so I went after that with all my might. It was in France that I received some of the most significant healing in my life. I released the chains of oppression and felt the spirit of depression leaving my body for good. My life was up and up from that point onward. I then left for my next adventure in South Korea, where I live now. It has taken me a long time to recover, but I am thankful to be where I am now. I still want to get a degree in education and to pursue educational research. Depression and anxiety have not stopped me from getting to where I want to be.

Recovery is Possible: You Just Have to stick with the Program

The moral of the story is that you can recover from mental illness. It is not something that you can deal with alone or in silence. You have to cope with it with the help of others. You need to have someone to lean on when the going gets tough. A doctor is a necessity for anyone struggling with mental illness. This is one of the key components of a good wellness program. I would urge anyone struggling with depression to seek medical treatment right away. Go to a doctor. Don't feel ashamed. Medicine and therapy are going to be key parts of your recovery journey, which can begin right away if you allow yourself to recover.

What is most important in healing from depression or living a life with mental illness is seeking help and sticking with the program. With mental illnesses, such as clinical depression and manic depression, you may need to have medication for the rest of your life. I had to deal with this reality as I talked to doctors about it. It was incredibly difficult to accept that I might have to live my life with medication forever; however, over the past decade, I've accepted it. The way to recover from mental illness was going to be to continue taking medicine. Moreover, I took medicine whenever I felt well, too.

I realized that I still needed to take medication during the good times. I'm not saying that everyone needs to take medication for depression. There are other ways you can deal with it. Some people choose to alter their diet or do CBT, and they can live their lives normally and in a healthy way. It's important that whenever you find something that works, keep doing it. Don't let it go when you feel well. That is one of the biggest mistakes you can make, thinking that when you're coasting with no worries, there's no need for treatment. That is a lie. Living with a mental illness requires long-term treatment in many cases to maintain overall health. I urge you to stay with your program and do everything you can to stay well.

Another Case Study

Daniella knew that she had to follow her doctor's advice and realized that it was important that she heed everything he had to say to her. Danielle had a depressive episode when she was younger, and she had to go into the hospital to get treatment for it. She spent over two weeks in the psychiatric ward of the local mental health clinic. It was a difficult time for her. She had to try many kinds of medicine for a year or two. Some worked, while others did not. It was a challenging time trying to come up with a solution. It tested her patience. All the while, Daniella believed that it was important that she try to do things that would be positive and enjoyable. She wanted to do her best to not beat herself up about her health condition and live the best life she could.

After one year, Daniella stayed on her program with medication and therapy treatment. She got better day by day and lived into each moment with joy. It was a difficult time while staying on medication, but Daniella knew that her doctor's advice was helping her to improve her life. In addition to medication and therapy, Daniella rode her bike to different places. She tried to get out as much she could. Knowing that exercise could help her moods, she tried to ride her bike to school, to the store, and other places. It allowed her to feel freer and more satisfied with her life. Additionally, she practiced meditation, which was helpful to getting her to a more stable life.

Above all, Daniella was happy to find a program that worked for her. Not everything works, but you must try everything you can before you settle on an actual program. Daniella was persistent to keep her doctor's advice and to do all things to help improve her life. In the end, she was successful in leading a life of healing.

Shortly after her healing, Daniella graduated from college and moved to Spain, where she worked as a bilingual administrative assistant. She could use her Spanish language skills to communicate with different people there.

She did not want to allow the mental illness to affect her life. Instead, she decided that she would do everything to complete her goals. She never lost sight of that. And through that whole period, she remained on her medication, did her exercise, meditated, and did everything she could to stay well. In the end, she was able to do everything she set her mind to, all because she kept on doing her wellness program, even when she felt well, and it made a huge difference. It gave her life and sustenance for a positive and uplifting future.

Conclusion

As you can see, recovering from mental illness takes a long time. I have experienced healing progressively over the past 14 years of living with a mental illness. Every year has gotten better, but it has not been without its struggles. Depression comes in phases and can come at times when work is heavy and free time is limited. Over time, it gets becomes easier to get out of depression when it hits hard. I learned that sticking with a program is one of the best ways to stay well and proactive about my mental health.

In a way, mental health requires the utmost vigilance and proactivity to stay healthy and safe. You cannot simply stay put and try to fight off the illness without some kind of protection or coping mechanism. If you don't have medication, CBT, talk therapy, or other strategies to deal with mental illness, you may not experience wellness. Instead, you will suffer. I don't want you to experience that. Instead, I want you to enjoy a life of meaning and wellness. Let my success story encourage you. I credit my faith, resilience, confidence, and other aspects with helping me stay well all these years. It is fantastic. I believe that anyone with a mental illness can heal and live a life of recovery. I hope that my story sheds light on how this is possible and that it encourages you to seek treatment and help so that you can be free from the bonds of this illness. All things are possible; you just have to seek help. Admit that you are weak and need some assistance. In weakness, there can be a strength that enables you to endure any circumstance. With help and recovery, healing and restoration follow.

6 DEALING WITH THE STIGMA OF MENTAL ILLNESS

In this chapter, I want to address a subject that is crucial to your understanding of mental illness because there are too many people who don't understand it and have certain prejudices against it. I want to discuss the stigmas attached to depression and anxiety and how I have fought to end those stigmas.

The Stigma of Mental Illness

There have been stigmas against mental illness for centuries. Many people thought that mentally handicapped people were dangerous and had to be institutionalized. Until the nineteenth century, there was no such thing as psychiatry. People suffered in silence and were unable to receive the treatment that would have enabled them to live a happy life while recovering from the condition. It is true that mental illness leads people to do dangerous things, including killing people in mass attacks. Unfortunately, people who have a mental illness such as depression have been some of the worst criminals, and they occasionally lose their lives over it in suicides, as well. Had they received some kind of treatment for their condition, things may have ended differently.

For generations, mental illness stigma has caused so many people to remain quiet and hide their illness. People have suffered without medication or CBT. Consequently, they led miserable lives. Depression impacted work and school. The depression or anxiety wreaked havoc in their lives so that they were unable to function or do the things that they needed to do. It is unfortunate. There are too many suicides every year because people are too afraid or proud to seek help for their condition.

I want to say this: mental health stigma kills. It is one of the worst killers of our time. Because there is a stigma, mental illness kills people every year.

They suffer in silence or kill themselves because no one extended a hand to help them and they didn't seek help. People quietly observe a person suffering and don't do anything about it because they are afraid to handle it or enter into their mess. But the thing is, people need help. They need someone to lean on. What we need more is mental health awareness and support that encourages people to seek clinical guidance they need to live a full and meaningful life. That is why I support the fight against mental health stigma in communities around the world.

Case Study

Studying and school are valuable in South Korea. Many people go to school and they are serious about studying. Students study an average of 14 hours per day, including in school, after school academy, and homework. They study sometimes until 10 pm or 11 pm at night, go to sleep at 1 or 2 am and then get up at 6 or 7 am. They are tired and worn out. Every year, to graduate from high school, students must take the Korean SAT test to get into university.

Students spend years preparing, cramming, and studying for this exam that determines their future. Their families spend thousands of dollars to put them through school and early adulthood. The investment is huge. And then, when some of them fail the test and all that studying goes to waste, thousands commit suicide. It is one of the saddest things.

South Korea struggles with the stigma against mental illness, too. It is one of the worst places to live with a mental illness, because mental health centers are non-existent, although there are some psychiatric clinics available. The notion of saving face has also caused the society to grow up with people who cannot express their emotions, which are repressed deep within them, causing them to grow up with a variety of unhealthy mental health conditions. It is all because there is a stigma against mental illness. Many people live in denial that there is a problem. Mothers don't want to admit their child has a mental health issue. They are fearful of the shame and social consequences of disclosing a mental illness. It is so sad.

Combating the Stigma in a Hostile World

Mental illness is something that is hard to deal with already. With millions of people around the world unable to express their emotions, there are many cases that are not dealt with professionally. Too many people go without treatment and their health and personal life suffer as a result. People live in denial and yet endure hardships every day because they never go to the doctor. I think that it is the responsibility of people living with mental illness, advocates, and other people to stand up for what is right. We need to fight the stigma in this hostile world. We must tell people that it is better to help a loved one in need than ignore them.

With social isolation already growing, people crowd social networks because they are starving for attention and interaction, yet these individuals are lonelier than ever. It is a growing problem. People do not communicate the way they used to. We use a smartphone for virtually all forms of communication, transaction, and entertainment.

People are lost in the technology and unable to get out of it. But then, they do not seek the treatment that they need to get better. So, things continue. They get worse. As soon as it is worse, people get sick and are unable to function. They are forced to go to the doctor who can help them recover. Worse yet, they must be admitted to a psychiatric hospital which helps them in dire circumstances. I have been fortunate enough not to have to deal with this, except for two times in my life when I was in my late teens. Those two experiences marked me for the rest of my life, and I hope to never again enter such a facility. However, the experience shaped me as I sought to deal with the disorder and share my recovery story.

Living with a mental illness can seem like a lonely battle. It's one that many people do not understand, especially the ones who don't have a problem. People may pity you and may not fully understand what you're going through. But you have to fight for your life sometimes. That includes getting people into your life and sharing your struggle with them.

The way to fight mental illness stigma is to get it out in the open. Visibility is one of the most important things we can do. For many, mental illness is an invisible illness that people don't understand because they can't see it. Unlike physical conditions such as the flu, a cold, a broken arm, or something else, mental illness is invisible.

We cannot see someone's brain and how they are thinking. Someone may look perfectly okay on the outside, but inwardly, they are suffering - or even dying. We cannot know that for sure unless we find out. Therefore, I urge you to tell people about your illness. You don't have to reveal it to everyone, just loved ones and friends. You could even share it with your employer if you want or need accommodation. That may take some time to disclose. Ultimately, it is vital that you find ways to reveal your illness to those around you. If they don't know about it, there is no way they can help you. If you continue to hide in silence, you may never receive the healing that you desire. Fighting the stigma is what will save your life. Tell someone what's going on, whether that is a trusted friend, pastor, or another person you can talk to about it. Mental illness is a difficult battle, and it requires us to look outside ourselves and think about how others can assist us through the struggle because we all need help. Admittedly, this takes some time. You may feel shy or unable to express what you're feeling, but it is important that you find a way to get your illness out, because then, you can recover and thrive.

My Journey of Dealing with the Stigma

My personal journey with dealing with stigma has been marked by the internal shame that I have had as a result of living with depression and anxiety. Deep within me, I struggled with it and had a hard time with the stigma of depression for a while, because I felt a deep sense of what it meant for me. I did not want to admit that I had a problem and didn't want to tell anyone about it.

Gradually, I fought off the stigma by thinking to myself, "What would other people think about it?" I stopped asking myself that question and started thinking instead, "If people know about it, then they may want to help and see that living with a mental illness is a fight that we can overcome together as a team." I realized how much I needed to educate people about how to deal with the stigma attached to mental illness. I also overcame my personal pride that made me refuse help from others. Furthermore, I realized that I needed help from others to get me on the path to where I needed to be.

Admittedly, it has taken more than ten years to reach maturity and accept the fact that I sometimes struggle with depression. With medication and therapy, I realize what it has taken to get where I am now. I wanted to be well: that was my goal. If get well, I can live a life full of freedom and joy. But until that time, I must continually seek treatment and support from medical professionals who know more than I do about mental illness. It is, after all, something that affects the brain, it is complex and highly individualized. Therefore, I advise you to find ways to deal with depression that fits your own journey and help you recover. It's not something I can prescribe for anyone. Your doctor and therapist are the ones to consult for a long-term path that will lead to recovery. You must overcome the stigma attached to having a mental illness so you can be well in every respect.

Conclusion

Mental health stigma has been the source of many of society's problems. It has been an issue for some time, and it continues to plague our world today. If only society could accept mental illness for what it is, a real issue, then we could get the help we need.

Fortunately, things are getting better. People are talking about it. Celebrities like Catherine Zeta-Jones and Carrie Fisher have been outspoken survivors of mental illness. They want to talk about it because they think it is necessary for people to know about it. Their efforts are laudable, but I would urge you, as an average person, to stand up for what is right. Stand with the people who are suffering in silence across the globe. Advocate for them. Mental health needs a voice and it needs visibility. The revelation of individual struggles will help people recover. We cannot attain this goal if we don't fight for the rights of the people struggling with mental health problems.

Depression cannot win in the end. It has caused people to lose their lives. Think of Robin Williams, who committed suicide while depressed. We cannot let others suffer like this. Instead, we must stand up for the rights of millions of people walking with this invisible illness. Let us walk forward in confidence that people can live healthy lives of wellness and fulfillment. That was my own personal journey. I believe that it can be your success story, as well. Seek help. Make yourself visible. It will save your life.

7 WELLNESS TIPS

In this final chapter I will talk about how you can live a life full of wellness and good health even with depression.

Now, we should go into the ways that you can stay healthy with depression and what can contribute to living a healthier lifestyle while having depression.

Dealing with depression involves preventive measures. That includes medication, CBT, therapy, and others. Many people who are depressed require long-term care, and that includes visits to the doctor. Others may only see the doctor in a time of crisis. Either way, you must come up with some precautions to keep you out of the hospital or doctor's office. Here are some things that you can do to help your emotional state from day to day.

Sleep

Many Americans don't get enough sleep, and consequently, their moods and everyday lives are affected. When you are chronically fatigued, you may not feel like doing anything and may not live a healthy lifestyle. The one thing that impacts your moods more than anything is how much sleep you get every night. Improve both the quality and quantity of your sleep each night to experience long-term care and results.

Aim for getting between 7 and 9 hours per night for the average adult. Some need more and some need less, but don't compromise on this point, because it could be the difference between a life of depression or well-being and good health. Sleep also enables us to enjoy our lives much more. If you want to avoid medication or a hospital bed, then I suggest you get enough sleep at night.

Case Study

Nathalie had a hard time sleeping at night. She often could not remember where she left her belongings because she was so sleep-deprived. As her sleep patterns became disrupted, she eventually realized that she had to get some help. She went to see the doctor to help her sort out the problems of her sleep. Her doctor told her that she needed to stop the caffeine intake, drink more water, and find ways to relax at home in the evenings. Although she tried these methods, Nathalie was unable to sleep at night and she needed to get some more help. She went to see the doctor once more, and he gave her some meditation exercises that could help her get to sleep at night. She tried some silent meditation in a dark, cold room. It helped her a lot. Pretty soon, she was feeling a lot better about her sleep, and she was able to get between 8 and 9 hours of sleep every night. It was a miracle!

Diet

Our diet is one of the most crucial factors for overall wellness. The more healthy foods we consume, the better we feel. The more unhealthy foods we consume, the more miserable we feel. Food is what makes the man or woman, so if you want to feel good and experience a good life, watch your diet.

Many Americans consume the worst foods for their health and more people are becoming overweight. It is a health crisis. Diabetes is becoming more prevalent. Additionally, people get less exercise. A healthy lifestyle requires a good diet, and that makes the biggest difference in overall health and well-being. By eating the right brain and heart foods, you can feel a lot better about yourself, and your body will look better. Diets that are rich in nutrients, vegetables, and fruits will help you live a better life. The old saying, "you are what you eat" applies in this case. Watch your diet and don't eat too many sweet, fatty, or carb-filled foods, because those won't help you with weight management. You will literally "eat your feelings," because you won't feel too much better about yourself afterward.

Case Study

Rhett was conscious of his dieting and how it was affecting his overall lifestyle. He was packing on the pounds and was always eating his feelings. He would have fried chicken and beer on most nights, while indulging in pizza and burgers most of the time. Inwardly, Rhett was suffering. He was miserable, because his diet was not doing a good job of keeping him healthy. Furthermore, he felt tired a lot and almost fell down at work one day because of his exhaustion. Little did Rhett know that his diet was killing him. It was also causing him to feel depressed, so he had to do something about it. He went to his doctor and confessed to having a terrible diet that was not helping his situation. His doctor recommended he find a diet that was not rich in fat or carbohydrates, so he tried a bunch of different diets. Finally, he came up with an idea. He thought that he could have a diet that was rich in fruits and vegetables. After that time, Rhett lost about 10 lbs, and he felt infinitely better about himself. He could look in the mirror and see that he was a beautiful person inside and out. It did wonders for his self-confidence.

Exercise

Getting enough exercise is on everyone's list of things to do, but how many of us honestly want to exercise? We often stay at home, binge on Netflix, have our TV dinner, and simply want to sit. We don't want to get out and about. Our laziness negatively affects our gut and our overall well-being. One of the things that you can do for yourself is get out there and exercise. Get up off the recliner and go out and do something because you cannot simply sit and do nothing.

Our society emphasizes that people must work too hard so much that they have no time for rest, and when they do, they simply do not do any kind of recreation. Instead, they sleep, watch the latest episode of Game of Thrones, or do other leisure activities. Find a sport that you like, whether that is an individual sport or some other thing to help you to get into a healthier state. For example, if you like running, go for a run in the park. Or if you like to swim, pay a visit to the local pool and swim some laps. Like basketball? Join a local club so you can get your exercise in and feel loads better. Choose an exercise that suits your unique talents. Not everyone is made the same way, so find something you enjoy and stick with it. Don't feel you need to go to the gym to feel fit in your life. Instead, you pursue what gives you joy.

Case Study

Juliette was struggling with her weight and it was making her depressed. She also didn't have a healthy diet ort have many friends. Moreover, she struggled in her studies at the local university. It created a difficult situation. Juliette deeply desired to feel better and have a healthier lifestyle, but unfortunately, she couldn't get enough of her pumpkin spice lattes, chocolate brownies, and cheesecake. One of her friends named Rachel came up to her and said, "Juliette, why don't you try the Keto diet? I've heard that does wonders for your immune system and enables you to lose lots of weight!" Juliette said, "Why not?" So, Juliette tried the Keto diet and after about 4 weeks, she lost 15 lbs. It was amazing! She said, "I'm so glad I found something that works, because I feel great!" Juliette was a happy woman. She found meaning in her life and felt that her self-confidence had grown a lot. When she looked at herself in the mirror, she complimented herself and felt that she could truly love herself. It was the first time that she had ever experienced that. It was a memorable time for her.

Talk Therapy: Friendships

One of the most important things that we can do is cultivate good relationships with others. Depression dwells when people suffer alone, without the help of friends or close relationships. What you sometimes need more than anything is a friend you can lean on in times of trouble. We need to have good friendships because that is one of the best relationships we can have. In my life, I have found that my friendships have contributed to my well-being. Because I have continually been supported by close friends, I have been able to thrive in difficult situations. Friends can be life-giving, whether you are married or single.

Spending time with friends is a great strategy to help in your fight against depression. Therefore, I would highly advise you to seek friendships that will change your life. Good friends enable you to live a healthier and more fulfilled life. And when you're depressed or lonely, you have these friends for support and sustenance, because no one can live in isolation. As John Donne said, "No man is an island." Moreover, we need communities of people who can be the foundation of relationships that sustain people across the country.

Case Study

Oscar isolated himself from others and tended to not get involved with any relationship. But deep within himself, he was lonelier than ever. He used his smartphone all the time to communicate with his peers and friends. He was glued to the smartphone, whether he was on the subway or at school. He never seemed to get off his phone. Clearly, it was an addiction that he was struggling with. Oscar wanted to make friends, but he was afraid of what others might think of him. He also struggled with a speech impediment, making it difficult for him to talk. Therefore, he found it much easier to communicate through text message instead of actually talking to people. Oscar started to feel depressed, because he did not have any "real" friends. He had a ton of virtual friends on Facebook and in other apps. But how many real friends did he have? Not even one. He couldn't even lift one finger on his hand. It was so sad. Oscar wanted to have friends, but he didn't want to leave the safety and comfort of his apartment.

One day, Oscar was invited to a party by some friends at school. Oscar usually declined invitations to parties, because he didn't want to stutter and struggle to communicate with others around him. For this one time, Oscar wanted to go. He thought, "I don't want to have a FOMO (fear of missing out) anymore. I must have courage to face my fears. My friends invited me for a reason, so I should follow through and accept the invitation this time."

That day, Oscar decided to go to the party. He had fun. Although he stuttered with some of the people he was talking to, he didn't feel that it was causing him any pain. Nobody cared. Everyone was understanding of his situation, and no one wanted to laugh at him or make him feel ashamed of himself. It was great that he could be surrounded by people who were caring and compassionate. You don't normally get that kind of treatment. After that time, Oscar felt better. He felt more confident to accept invitations from people to go to parties and hang out. Later, he lost his self-consciousness attached to his speech impediment, and he was able to completely overcome it. The depression cloud totally lifted above his shoulders.

Having a Positive Attitude Makes Every Difference

Finally, it is vital that we find ways to be positive every day. Be thankful and express gratitude for what you have. This will make a difference in how you can live a happier and fulfilled life. Positive psychology has proven health benefits because it frees you from anxiety and depression. The more we can be positive with ourselves and others, the more endorphins and happy feelings we can produce.

Finding healthy ways to express our complex emotions can likewise be a vital part of our journey. If we feel angry, we should channel ways to get rid of the anger constructively. Finding outlets for our emotions, whether through creative arts or other ways, is valuable for our overall health. I encourage you to become more aware of your emotions and how you can deal with them using a positive approach.

There is too much negativity in the world today. We see it plastered all over the news, and there is no wonder that everyone feels depressed. I don't even like to watch the news anymore, because of the negative news. What better way to counter all the negativity in the world than to be positive? I want to be a positive world changer because I want to bring out the best in others and show how we can find light in the midst of darkness. That is the way keep me from being depressed. Being hopeful and resolving to be well keep me going. I think that anyone can get to this point if they work hard toward the goal and believe in healing and wholeness.

Case Study

Kenneth struggled to be positive all the time in the office. He was surrounded by Negative Nancies, who were griping about every new change that was happening. The thing he struggled to do was look on the bright side of things. His pay was low, his boss was a total jerk and autocrat, who took all measures into his own hands and did not consult or check with subordinates, and he felt miserable all the time. The negative energy was life-sucking, and Kenneth wanted to desperately move on and leave this job. Unfortunately, he did not have a lot of options at his disposal. He wasn't able to get another job, because the job market was flooded with applicants with his profile with very few openings. The job he had was in a sector with decreasing opportunities in business management. This situation created a significant hardship for Kenneth's life. As a result, he felt burdened under the weight of everything.

In the end, what made Kenneth become a positive person was surrounding himself with other positive influences in the office. That included his best colleague friend, who supported him through the difficult times. The two often did things for each other, had lunch together, and spent time supporting one another in all situations. They became really close so that they became best friends. Having a best buddy was one of the most important parts of Kenneth's life. A man or woman needs to have good friends. Especially for men, friendship has been neglected. More and more men are lonely. What made this important was that Kenneth could overcome his situation and have a friend who had his back. This aspect kept him positive and willing to go through the trials of having a negative workspace. Without his buddy, the path would have been much more difficult. Since he had a friend whom he could trust, Kenneth felt happy and satisfied with his life. It made a huge difference in his overall morale and standing at the company.

Wrapping Things Up

As you can see, there are various strategies you can try to develop a wellness program that can help you fight depression. We all need to focus on how we can better ourselves. Dealing with depression requires special attention and care, especially when it comes to sleep, diet, and exercise. Likewise, having helpful relationships and a positive attitude will enable you to live a healthier and more productive life. You just might be able to avoid getting into a depressive cycle again, if only for a day or two. Miracles happen every day. Believe that all things are possible.

CONCLUSION

Depression continues to plague the people of the United States. With more individuals diagnosed with mental illness every year, people continue to suffer, and still more don't dare speak up about their condition. It is a crisis that is affecting our country and we see how it is impacting society. Increased social network interaction and negative news have caused people to spiral into despair. Our world is hurting and there are millions of people who need help but are not seeking it.

This book can help you understand depression and how to cope and thrive. Things can only get better. Depression may affect us once in our lives, or it may persistently knock at our mind's door if we are not careful and vigilant in taking care of ourselves. To thrive with good mental health, you have to be willing to fight for it. You need to have strategies going forward, whether that is exercise, prayer, meditation, or a better diet.

The only way you're going to be able to endure in times of adversity is to give yourself the time and space to understand your condition and learn what causes you to slip. Then you can treat the condition with measures that will help you avoid depressive episodes.

Treat the condition by understanding your early warning signs. Be aware of when things start to unravel so that you can quickly get the help you need.

How do you manage your symptoms and lead a life of wellness? In my opinion, you have to do the right things for yourself. You must be kind to yourself and show love to yourself more than to any other person. Get the right amount of exercise, eat well, sleep a lot, and have a supportive group of friends. These are the things that will help you recover and be well again.

Have enough positive influence in our lives to help us think positively. As you consider your next steps, believe that things will get better. Trust that this one depressive episode is only temporary. The cloud will lift. Allow yourself to live a life full of happiness. This is the Depression Code.

JACK WILSON

www.ingramcontent.com/pod-product-compliance
Lightning Source LLC
Chambersburg PA
CBHW071256070526
44583CB00017B/2490